THE VEIL BETWEEN

The Veil Between

DEMETRI WELSH

CONTENTS

To those who've dared to peer into the darkness and saw themselves staring back.

This book is for the restless souls who question everything, the ones unafraid to pull at the threads of reality until it unravels. To the lost, the broken, the haunted—this is for you. Let the shadows guide you home.

INTRODUCTION: WHEN THE VEIL THINS

The thing about reality is that most people take it at face value. They move through life with blinders on, accepting what they see, feel, and touch as solid, concrete truths. The world is measured in inches, the mind contained within the skull, and the soul—a nebulous idea they tuck away for their pastor or priest to handle on Sundays. But what happens when that framework begins to crack? What happens when you see something that shouldn't be there, feel something crawl across your skin that isn't visible to the naked eye, or wake up in the middle of the night to find a shadow standing at the foot of your bed?

Welcome to the cracks in the foundation.

This isn't just a book. It's a key—a map to the realms that exist between the fibers of your everyday life. The forgotten places where spirits roam, where the dead don't stay dead, and where energies and entities you've never been taught to recognize are living just beyond the veil. And I'm not talking about Hollywood ghosts with rattling chains or the watered-down version of the afterlife you were spoon-fed as a kid. What you're about to step into is something much darker, much older, and much more terrifying than you've ever imagined.

The universe is not what you think it is. We're not living in a world divided by clean lines of the physical and the spiritual, the living and the dead, the material and the ethereal. No. Our reality is a woven tapestry, and that threadbare fabric has holes. Holes that open and close without warning. Holes that let things in—things that shouldn't be here. I've seen them. Hell, I've felt them. And once you do too, you'll never be the same.

You've heard the term "haunted" thrown around casually, haven't you? Maybe even laughed at it. "Oh, that house is haunted," someone will say, as though it's some harmless idea, a fun Halloween scare. But haunted doesn't just mean there are spirits around. No, being haunted is more insidious than that. To be haunted means that something has attached itself to you, that something has marked you as its playground, its food source, its fascination. It's the whispers in your ear at night when you're half asleep, the cold spots in your room that never seem to go away, and the way you suddenly feel drained after being alone in a perfectly quiet room.

What we're dealing with here are parasites, astral leeches, and entities that make their way into your life by feeding on the one thing they crave most—your energy. These beings aren't friendly. They aren't misunderstood. They're predators. And guess what? They're not bound by the same rules that govern you and me. These things exist beyond the realm of time, beyond the boundaries of space. They slip between worlds, through dimensions, and sometimes, they latch on.

And then there's the shadow people. You've heard of them, I'm sure. Shadow figures that stand at the edge of your peripheral vision, watching, waiting. Maybe you've seen one before—thought it was just a trick of the light, maybe an overactive imagination. But I'm here to tell you that they're real. More real than the ground beneath your feet. They've been watching humanity for centuries, slipping through the cracks in our dimension like predators stalking prey. What do they want? Why do they appear only to certain people? And most terrifyingly, what happens if they decide to follow you?

These questions might already be creeping up your spine as you read, but it's about to get worse. The afterlife—let's talk about that, shall we? We've been fed this comforting narrative for centuries, haven't we? Heaven and hell, angels and demons, a cosmic balance of light and dark. It's all bullshit. The truth is much more twisted. The afterlife is not a neatly ordered system with pearly gates and fire pits. It's a marketplace, a battleground, a place where souls are bartered, traded, and consumed. Imagine that—the very essence of who you are, sold to the highest bidder in a cosmic war you didn't even know you were part of.

And here's the kicker—this isn't just about belief. It's not about whether you think ghosts exist, or whether you've ever had a paranormal experience. This is about science. Modern science is only beginning to scratch the surface of what ancient esoteric teachings have known for millennia. Quantum physics is revealing that reality is not the solid, immovable construct we've been taught. Time isn't linear, space isn't fixed, and matter isn't solid. It's all in flux. And in those fluxes, in those gaps, the things that shouldn't exist slip through.

I've spent my life exploring the dark corners of this world and the next. I've seen things I can't unsee. Experienced things that no rational explanation can touch. I've been marked, followed, drained, and haunted in ways that would make most people lose their fucking minds. But I've also learned how to navigate these waters. How to protect myself. How to fight back.

This book is a journey into those shadows. We're going to explore the science of spirits and the metaphysical truths hidden behind centuries of dogma. We'll dive into the astral plane and the entities that feed there. We'll examine shadow people, not as figments of imagination but as interdimensional predators stalking the weak points of our reality. And we're going to rip the lid off the sanitized version of the afterlife you've been taught to believe in and expose it for what it truly is—a grotesque marketplace where souls are traded like fucking cattle.

So, buckle up. This isn't a casual read, and it's not for the faint of heart. I'm not here to entertain you with spooky stories. I'm here to pull back the veil and show you what's lurking on the other side. Once you've seen it, you won't be able to unsee it. The shadows will take on a new meaning, the flicker in the corner of your eye won't just be a trick of the light anymore, and when you feel that cold shiver run down your spine, you'll know.

The veil between worlds is thinning, and what's on the other side is hungry.

Are you ready to face it?

| 1 |

Chapter One: The Quantum Spirit Theory

Let me paint you a picture. Imagine you're sitting alone in your room, the lights dim, the world outside your window slipping into silence. Maybe you're scrolling through your phone, maybe you're lost in thought, but there's a moment—a fleeting instant—where something feels *off*. You can't put your finger on it. The air seems to shift, just slightly. A chill, maybe. A sense that something, or someone, is in the room with you. You look up. Nothing. You're alone, or at least, you think you are. But the feeling doesn't leave. It lingers, crawling over your skin, seeping into your mind.

That, my friend, is the first crack in the fabric of your reality.

For as long as we've been human, we've lived within the confines of the tangible world. We wake up, we eat, we breathe, we sleep. We've been trained to accept what we see as the only truth. But what if I told you that this physical world we cling to is nothing more than a fraction of what actually exists? That what you can see, touch, and hear is just a thin layer over something much more chaotic and unpredictable.

And what if I told you that the science we've been taught all our lives—the mathematics, the physics, the rules of reality—are only telling part of the story?

This is where things get terrifying, because science is starting to catch up with what spiritual and metaphysical practitioners have known for centuries: that the world as we know it isn't as stable as we thought. Quantum physics, once a fringe field of study, is beginning to reveal a darker, more unsettling truth about our existence.

The Uncertainty of Reality

The quantum world is fucking weird. That's the scientific term for it. It doesn't follow the rules we've been taught. Particles can exist in two places at once. Time doesn't flow in one direction. The smallest building blocks of the universe aren't solid objects; they're clouds of probability, flickering in and out of existence based on whether or not they're being observed.

In the quantum world, reality itself seems to bend to the will of the observer. What you see, what you experience, isn't necessarily what's *there*. And that's where things get dangerous. You see, the quantum realm doesn't just apply to the smallest particles in the universe. It's the very foundation of reality itself.

What we experience as reality—the walls of your room, the ground beneath your feet, even your own body—is made up of these quantum particles. But these particles are not solid. They're not fixed. They're always shifting, always in flux, always hovering between being and non-being.

So, what the fuck does that mean for you?

It means that the world you think is so real, so solid, is actually more like a hologram. A simulation of sorts, one that's constantly fluctuating between existence and nonexistence. The space between you and the walls of your room? It's not empty. It's filled with potential, with energy, with particles that blink in and out of being faster than you can comprehend.

Now, here's where the metaphysical comes crashing into the scientific. If reality is so unstable at its very core, what's stopping other forms of existence from bleeding through? If the fabric of the universe is so fragile, so prone to tearing, then what else is lurking just beyond that thin veil, waiting to slip through when no one is looking?

The Unseen Dimensions

We're getting into the deep shit now. Quantum theory suggests that there are multiple dimensions—realms that exist parallel to ours, vibrating at different frequencies, just out of reach. And this isn't just some sci-fi, tinfoil-hat bullshit. This is real science, backed by some of the most brilliant minds in physics.

These other dimensions could be as real as ours, but we simply lack the ability to perceive them. They're vibrating at a different frequency, outside the range of our senses. But that doesn't mean they're not there.

In fact, every once in a while, these dimensions can overlap. Like two radio stations bleeding into each other on a faulty signal, they can intersect, allowing things from one realm to slip into the other. And here's the horrifying part—what if some of the beings that exist in those other dimensions are far more ancient, far more malevolent, than anything we've ever encountered?

The Science of Spirits

Let's talk about spirits. Ghosts, entities, apparitions—whatever you want to call them. Most people write them off as hallucinations, tricks of the mind, or, at worst, figments of superstition. But what if I told you that these so-called "ghosts" are not only real but that science can explain their existence?

Think about it. If quantum particles can blink in and out of existence, if entire dimensions can bleed into ours, why couldn't spirits—beings made of energy—exist in a similar way? What if ghosts are not trapped souls or dead people wandering the Earth, but rather, echoes from other dimensions? Or worse—what if they're intelligent entities, living in these parallel dimensions, crossing into ours when the quantum walls between us weaken?

In quantum theory, energy is never destroyed. It simply changes form. When a person dies, their physical body decays, but what happens to their energy? What happens to that spark of consciousness? Is it possible that this energy lingers, drifting between dimensions, trapped in a liminal space where the laws of physics no longer apply?

Entities in the Cracks

Now that you've wrapped your head around the idea that reality isn't as solid as it seems, let me introduce you to something far more disturbing: the entities that exist within the cracks of our world. These aren't your friendly neighborhood ghosts. They're not the spirits of loved ones trying to send you messages from beyond. These are predators—astral parasites—creatures that exist in the spaces between dimensions, feeding on the energy of the living.

The most common type of entity people encounter are what I call "leech spirits." These things attach themselves to people like a parasite, draining their energy slowly over time. They're drawn to trauma, to fear, to sadness. When you're at your lowest, when your energy is fractured and weak, that's when they strike. You might not see them, but you can feel them. That cold chill that creeps up your spine when you're alone. That heavy feeling of dread that seems to come out of nowhere. They're there, lurking just out of sight, feeding.

And it gets worse. There are stories, passed down through ancient spiritual traditions, of entities far more dangerous than leeches. These creatures don't just feed on your energy—they take over. They're opportunistic, waiting for a moment of vulnerability, a crack in your defenses. When they find it, they slip inside, like a virus infecting a cell, and they don't let go. These entities have been called by many names throughout history—demons, jinn, malevolent spirits—but their goal is always the same: to take control, to consume.

A Fractured Reality

We've been taught to believe that the world is a safe, stable place. That what we see is all there is. But the truth is far more terrifying. Reality is fragile. It's a thin veil stretched over something much darker, much older, and much more malevolent than we've ever been told.

Quantum physics is proving what spiritual practitioners have known for centuries—that there are cracks in the fabric of existence, and in those cracks, things exist that defy explanation. Beings made of energy, parasites that feed on the living, and entities from other dimensions that slip through when we least expect it.

And here's the thing—you can feel it. You've felt it. Every time you've experienced that creeping dread, every time you've seen something out of the corner of your eye, every time you've woken up in the middle of the night with the sensation that someone or something was watching you—it wasn't your imagination. It wasn't a trick of the mind. It was real.

Reality is not what you think it is. The walls that separate us from the unknown are thin. And as science continues to unravel the mysteries of the quantum world, it's becoming clear that the veil between our dimension and others is far more porous than we ever realized.

So, the next time you feel that chill, the next time you sense something in the room with you, remember: it's not just in your head. Something is out there. Something is waiting. And the cracks in reality are getting wider.

Welcome to the quantum nightmare.

| 2 |

Chapter Two: Astral Parasites – Energy Vampires

Let me ask you something. Have you ever woken up after what should've been a full night's sleep, but you felt like you hadn't rested at all? Maybe you've gone through phases in your life where everything seems heavier. Your limbs feel like lead, your thoughts are clouded, and no matter how much coffee you down or how much sleep you get, you just can't shake that bone-deep fatigue. Sure, life is exhausting. But sometimes, it's not just life dragging you down.

Sometimes, something is feeding on you.

In this chapter, we're going deep into the realm of astral parasites—those unseen, vampiric entities that latch onto your energy and suck the life out of you slowly, sometimes so slowly that you don't even notice it until you're completely depleted. These things are worse than any ghost or haunting. They're not here to scare you. They don't make noise. They don't slam doors. They don't show themselves in any way that's obvious. They're predators of a different sort—silent, patient, and relentless. They don't want your attention. They just want your life force.

And chances are, you've encountered them before.

The Nature of Astral Parasites

First, let's get one thing straight. When I talk about astral parasites, I'm not talking about your standard movie demons or spirits. I'm not even talking about your run-of-the-mill hauntings where a spirit might knock a picture off the wall or make the temperature drop. No, these parasites are something far more insidious.

Astral parasites are energy-based entities that exist in the invisible realms surrounding us—the astral plane, to be precise. Think of them as interdimensional leeches, or even viruses, floating in a sea of human consciousness and energy, waiting for an opportunity to latch onto an unsuspecting host. These entities are not bound by the same physical laws as we are. They operate on a different frequency, a different level of existence, but they can—and do—cross into our plane when the conditions are right.

They feed off human energy, plain and simple. The way we feed off food, they feed off life force. Your emotions, your vitality, your mental clarity—these are all things they crave. And they don't need an invitation to attach themselves to you. Unlike the old vampire legends, where you had to welcome them in, astral parasites can attach to anyone whose energy is vulnerable, weakened, or fractured. They don't discriminate. If your aura is cracked—maybe from trauma, grief, stress, or even just exhaustion—they'll slip in, unnoticed, and start siphoning off your energy.

The worst part? Most people don't even know they're being drained. You might just feel tired, or foggy, or emotionally numb. You might even start to feel like you're losing your grip on reality, but you chalk it up to stress or a bad day. In reality, these parasites could be clinging to you, sinking their hooks into your energy and feeding without you ever knowing.

But once they're in, getting rid of them isn't easy.

How They Attach Themselves

So, how do these parasites get to you? What makes someone a target? Let me break it down for you.

Astral parasites are opportunistic. They look for cracks in your aura, the energy field that surrounds your physical body. Your aura is supposed to act as a shield, a barrier that protects you from outside energies. But like anything, it can weaken. Life takes its toll, right? Trauma, stress, heartbreak, depression, even physical illness can all weaken your aura. It's like walking around with an open wound—if your aura is torn or weakened, it leaves you vulnerable.

And that's where the parasites come in.

Emotional trauma is one of their favorite entry points. When you've experienced something that tears you apart emotionally—whether it's the death of a loved one, a nasty breakup, or a period of deep, prolonged depression—your aura can fracture. You become a beacon to these entities. They can sense your vulnerability, your lowered defenses, and they'll latch onto that crack in your energy like a mosquito biting through skin.

But they're not just attracted to sadness. Anger, fear, anxiety—these are all emotions that weaken the aura and create an opening for astral parasites. In fact, negative emotions are like a fucking buffet for these entities. They feed on low vibrations, which is why people who are caught in a cycle of negative thinking or emotional turmoil are prime targets.

Ever notice how when you're going through something particularly tough in life, things seem to spiral out of control? One bad thing after another? That's not just bad luck. These parasites latch onto you when you're down, and they *keep* you down. They thrive on your suffering, and the more you suffer, the more they drain from you.

But it's not just emotional pain that attracts them. Physical illness can do the same thing. When your body is weak, your aura weakens as well, and that's when they move in. If you've ever experienced long-term illness or even just felt like your recovery was unusually slow, it's possible that something more than just your physical health was at play. Astral parasites can linger around hospitals, hospice care centers, and places where sickness and death are common. It's like a hunting ground for them.

And once they've attached themselves to you, they can be a real bitch to shake.

The Symptoms of Being Drained

So how do you know if you're being fed on by one of these astral parasites? It's not like they leave bite marks or bruises. Their attacks are subtle, almost impossible to detect at first. But over time, the signs become clearer.

1. **Chronic Fatigue:** This is one of the most common symptoms. I'm not talking about feeling tired because you stayed up late or had a long day at work. I'm talking about a deep, bone-weary exhaustion that no amount of sleep can cure. You wake up tired, go through your day in a fog, and by the time you hit the pillow at night, you're still just as drained. This is because the parasite is feeding on your life force, siphoning off your energy bit by bit.

2. **Emotional Numbness:** People who are under the influence of an astral parasite often report feeling emotionally flat. Nothing excites you. Nothing makes you happy, sad, or even angry.

It's like your emotions are being sucked out of you, leaving you hollow inside. This is because the parasite is feeding on your emotional energy, leaving you a shell of your former self.

3. **Unexplained Anxiety or Depression:** Some parasites feed specifically on emotional turmoil, and they can amplify negative feelings. You might start feeling anxious for no reason or fall into a deep depression that doesn't seem to have a cause. This is the parasite manipulating your energy, stirring up negative emotions so it can feed.

4. **Nightmares and Sleep Disturbances:** Many people who are being drained by these entities report vivid nightmares, especially ones involving dark figures, shadowy presences, or being chased. The parasites seem to be most active at night, feeding while you sleep, which can also result in restless nights or frequent waking.

5. **Physical Symptoms:** In some cases, the energy drain can manifest as physical ailments. Frequent headaches, muscle aches, and a general feeling of unwellness are common. These aren't symptoms you can easily explain away. It's as if your body is under constant stress, even when there's no external reason for it.

6. **A Feeling of Being Watched:** This is one of the creepiest symptoms. People who are dealing with astral parasites often report feeling like they're being watched, especially when they're alone. It's a constant, unsettling sensation of being observed, even when no one else is around.

If any of this sounds familiar, you might already have something clinging to you.

How They Feed

Astral parasites don't just drain energy like flicking a switch. They're much more subtle than that. They feed slowly, over time, like a vampire that takes just enough blood to keep you alive but always weak. They're patient, methodical. They'll drain you just enough to keep you functioning, but never fully rested, never fully energized.

They feed on your emotional and physical energy, but they also feed on your thoughts. Your fears. Your doubts. They whisper to you, amplify your insecurities, and make you feel small, weak, and helpless. They thrive on despair. And the more despair you feel, the more they can take.

Some parasites will even create situations in your life that cause more stress, more drama, more pain—because that's the energy they feed on. They manipulate events around you, twist your thoughts, and influence your behavior in ways that create the exact emotional turmoil they crave. It's a vicious cycle.

The worst part? Most people go through their entire lives never realizing what's happening to them. They chalk it up to bad luck, chronic illness, or depression. They see doctors, therapists, and healers, but nothing works. Because the root cause isn't something physical or psychological—it's something much darker. Something unseen.

Breaking Free

Here's the good news: you don't have to live like this forever. Once you know what you're dealing with, you can fight back. Getting rid of an astral parasite isn't easy, but it's possible. And it starts with awareness.

The first step is recognizing the signs, acknowledging that you're being drained. Once you do that, you can take action to repair your energy, to strengthen your aura, and to sever the connection these entities have to you. But it's not as simple as just burning sage or say-ing a prayer. You have to do the work. You have to face the darkness head-on.

Cleansing rituals, energy work, and spiritual protection techniques are all critical tools for battling these parasites. But the most important thing is taking back your power. These entities feed on weakness, on fear, and on despair. The stronger you become—mentally, emotionally, and spiritually—the less appealing you are to them. Strengthen your aura, clear your mind, and start living with intention. When you do, they'll have no choice but to move on to an easier target.

But never forget—they're out there, waiting, watching, and they're always hungry.

Are you strong enough to keep them at bay?

| 3 |

Chapter Three: Shadow Beings and Predators

There's a moment—a flicker in the corner of your eye—where you swear you saw something move, but when you turn your head, there's nothing there. Just empty space. A trick of the light, right? Your brain playing games with you. It happens again, though. Another flicker, another shadow darting just beyond the edge of your vision. The rational part of your mind brushes it off. But deep down, in the part of your gut that knows better, a chill starts to creep up your spine. You've felt it before. That quiet, gnawing sensation that something *is* there, something lurking in the periphery of your reality, just beyond what you can see.

That feeling? It's not paranoia. It's not an overactive imagination. It's not the stress of your daily life catching up to you. No, it's something much older, much darker, and far more dangerous.

What you've experienced is the first sign of the shadow beings.

They're real, and they've been watching us for centuries, maybe longer. They exist in the cracks between dimensions, slipping in and out of our world at will. They don't belong here, but they come anyway, and when they do, they don't come with good intentions. They come to watch, to feed, to manipulate. They are predators, not bound by the physical laws we understand, and they've been preying on us since the beginning of time.

What Are Shadow Beings?

Let's get one thing straight: shadow beings are not ghosts. They're not your deceased relatives coming to visit, nor are they the lingering spirits of the dead. They are something else entirely, something that doesn't belong to this world. In fact, they're not even from this dimension. Shadow beings are interdimensional entities—creatures that exist in the spaces between realities, the dark, forgotten corners of existence where our laws of physics don't apply.

The term "shadow" is key here. That's how they present themselves to us. We don't see them as they truly are because their true form can't fully exist in our dimension. Instead, what we see are dark, humanoid figures—blurry, black, and featureless. Often, they have no discernible faces, no eyes, no mouths. Just a silhouette. An outline. A void in the shape of a person. Sometimes they're tall, unnaturally tall, towering over everything in the room. Other times, they're small, hunched, crawling along the edges of your vision like insects skittering in the dark.

What they look like doesn't matter as much as what they *are*. And what they are, at their core, are predators.

Why They're Here

Why do these beings come here, to our dimension? What could they possibly want? The answers are simple and terrifying.

They come for two reasons: to feed and to manipulate.

Feeding: Shadow beings, much like astral parasites, feed on human energy. But unlike parasites, which are content to latch on and slowly drain your life force over time, shadow beings are more aggressive. They thrive on fear. They feed off the very essence of terror itself. That feeling of dread that washes over you when you're alone in the dark? That sudden spike of panic when you sense something lurking in the corner of your room? That's them. They create fear, amplify it, and then feed off it. Fear is their sustenance, and the more frightened you become, the more power they gain.

Manipulating: Shadow beings don't just want to feed. They want control. They are masters of psychological warfare, manipulating their targets with subtle, terrifying tactics. They prey on your deepest insecurities, your most primal fears. They don't need to speak to communicate; their presence alone is enough to plant seeds of doubt in your mind. Once they've established their presence in your life, they'll begin to twist your thoughts, your emotions, and your perception of reality itself. You might start to doubt your own sanity. You might begin to feel like you're losing control of your own thoughts. That's how they operate—through fear, confusion, and control.

What's worse, once they've got their hooks in you, they rarely let go.

The Watchers

There's a name that's been whispered about shadow beings for centuries: *The Watchers*. It's fitting. These entities seem to have an eerie, almost obsessive interest in humanity. They watch us. Sometimes from the corners of our vision, sometimes in full view, standing at the foot of your bed or in the dark hallway outside your room. But make no mistake—they're always watching.

What are they waiting for? Why do they observe so closely, so relentlessly?

Some theories suggest that shadow beings are collectors. They collect knowledge, studying human behavior, emotions, and fears. Others believe they are soldiers of a larger force, scouting our dimension for weaknesses, looking for openings to exploit. The truth is, no one knows for sure. Their motives remain as shadowy as their forms. But one thing is certain—they aren't benign observers. They're here for a reason, and that reason is not good.

Shadow People Encounters

The phenomenon of shadow people is more common than most people realize. You might have heard stories, or maybe you've even had your own experience. The details vary from case to case, but the core elements are always the same: a dark figure, a sense of being watched, and an overwhelming feeling of dread.

Let me tell you about a few encounters that will send chills down your spine.

Case 1: The Hat Man

The Hat Man is one of the most notorious types of shadow beings. Witnesses report seeing a tall, shadowy figure wearing a wide-brimmed hat. His silhouette is always the same—tall, imposing, with a hat that obscures his head. Some people see him standing at the foot of their bed. Others see him in doorways, or lurking in the corners of dark rooms. He never speaks. He doesn't need to. His presence alone is enough to induce terror.

One woman, let's call her Lisa, described her encounter with the Hat Man in vivid detail. She woke up in the middle of the night, unable to move, her body frozen in place by an unseen force. Standing at the foot of her bed was the Hat Man. He didn't move, didn't make a sound, but the fear that washed over her was unlike anything she had ever felt before. She felt as though her very soul was being drained. The more she tried to scream, the more paralyzed she became, as if his very presence was sucking the life out of her. And just when she thought she couldn't take it anymore, he disappeared. But the fear? The fear never left.

Case 2: The Crawlers

Not all shadow beings stand tall and menacing. Some crawl. And those are the ones that really get under your skin—literally. Imagine waking up in the middle of the night, the room pitch black, only to see something moving along the floor. It's not an animal, not a person, but a shadow. A dark, creeping figure with elongated limbs, crawling on all fours like some kind of insect. That's exactly what happened to a man named Jared.

He had been waking up in the middle of the night for weeks, feeling like something was wrong. He couldn't explain it, just a gut feeling. Then, one night, he saw it. A shadowy figure, low to the ground, crawling toward him. Its movements were jerky, unnatural, almost insect-like. He froze in place, paralyzed with fear, as the creature crawled up onto his bed. It didn't touch him, didn't make a sound, but the fear was suffocating. Then, just as quickly as it had appeared, it was gone. Jared didn't sleep for days after that.

Case 3: The Lurkers

Sometimes, shadow beings don't even need to appear in full to create terror. Sometimes, they just linger at the edges of your vision, lurking, waiting. A woman named Samantha recounted her experiences with these shadow lurkers. It started with small things—feeling like someone was watching her while she worked late at night, sensing a presence in the room when she was alone. Then, she started seeing them. Dark shapes, just at the edge of her vision, darting away when she turned her head.

It escalated when one night she saw a shadow standing outside her bedroom door. Tall, featureless, just watching. She closed her eyes, trying to convince herself it wasn't real. But when she opened them again, the shadow was still there. It didn't move, didn't make a sound, but the sense of dread it brought with it was so intense she could barely breathe. She tried to get out of bed, but her legs wouldn't move. She was frozen, trapped under its gaze. And just when she thought she was going to pass out from fear, the shadow disappeared.

But the feeling of being watched never went away.

The Predator's Tactics

What makes shadow beings so dangerous isn't just their ability to feed on fear. It's the psychological games they play. They don't need to touch you to hurt you. They don't need to physically attack. They get inside your head. They manipulate your mind, your thoughts, your emotions.

They're patient. They'll haunt you for weeks, months, sometimes even years, slowly wearing you down. They want to break you, to make you doubt your own sanity. They want you to live in fear, because that's what gives them power. They thrive on terror, and the more you fear them, the stronger they become.

The worst part? You can't fight them the way you'd fight a normal threat. You can't hit them, can't run from them, can't hide. They exist in a space that's beyond the physical, and they don't play by the rules we understand. And that's what makes them so terrifying. You can't see them coming. You can't predict their next move.

All you can do is survive.

Fighting Back

So how do you fight back against something that isn't even fully in our dimension? It's not easy, but it's not impossible either.

The first step is understanding what they are. Knowledge is power. Once you understand that shadow beings feed on fear, you can start to take that power back. Fear is their weapon, and if you can learn to control it, you take away their food source.

Easier said than done, I know. Fear is a primal instinct, hardwired into our brains for survival. But shadow beings aren't natural predators. They're dimensional intruders, and they don't belong here. That means they can be repelled.

Spiritual protection is key. Strengthening your aura, clearing your space, and using protective rituals can help create a barrier between you and these entities. Sage, crystals, salt—tools used by ancient cultures to ward off negative energies—can be effective. But the most important weapon you have is your own strength of will. Shadow beings feed on weakness, on insecurity. The stronger your mind, the more resilient your spirit, the less power they have over you.

But always remember, they're still out there. Watching. Waiting. Lurking in the dark corners of your reality.

The next time you catch a glimpse of something out of the corner of your eye, don't dismiss it so quickly. It might not be your imagination. It might be one of them, standing there, just beyond the veil.

Watching.

| 4 |

Chapter Four: The Afterlife Market – Soul Currency

What if I told you that everything you've been taught about the afterlife is a lie? Heaven and Hell? Sure, those ideas have been comforting to billions over the centuries, but let's be real for a second—they were designed to keep people in line, to keep the masses obedient and afraid. What we're told about what happens after we die is all about control. Control of your actions, your beliefs, your soul. But here's the terrifying truth: the afterlife isn't some neatly divided realm of angels with harps and demons with pitchforks. It's far more disturbing than that.

The afterlife is a market. And your soul? It's the currency.

In this chapter, we're ripping the lid off the sanitized, fairytale version of what happens after death. No pearly gates, no eternal paradise for the righteous, and no fiery pits for the wicked. What really happens is a system of exchange—an economy of souls—where spirits are traded, harvested, and used as energy in ways you couldn't begin to comprehend. And the kicker? Most people have no idea this is happening. You've been led to believe that your actions in life determine where you go after death. But what if your soul is just a commodity, no different than a dollar bill, a piece of gold, or a stock on the market? What if the afterlife is a cosmic battleground, a market where souls are bought and sold like cattle?

Let's get into it. You're not going to like what you find.

The Soul as Energy

Before we get into the actual trading, let's talk about what a soul *is*. We all have some vague idea of the soul—a spark of life, a piece of your true self, the core of who you are. But what is a soul in the metaphysical sense? Here's the raw truth: your soul is energy. Pure, unfiltered, raw energy. It's the most valuable resource in existence. And like any energy source—like oil, electricity, or gold—it can be used, stored, and most disturbingly, exploited.

Everything in existence is built on energy. Our physical bodies, our emotions, our thoughts—all are forms of energy. But the soul? That's something different. It's the fuel that powers your consciousness, the thing that keeps you tethered to this reality. And when you die, that energy doesn't just disappear. It doesn't evaporate or fade into the ether. It has to go somewhere.

And that's where the afterlife comes in. But not in the way you think.

The Lie of Heaven and Hell

Religions have painted the afterlife in black and white terms for millennia. You do good things, you go to Heaven. You sin, you end up in Hell. Simple, right? But this dualistic vision of the afterlife is nothing more than a convenient story to keep people afraid of stepping out of line. Think about it—what better way to control people than by making them believe that their eternal soul is at risk for punishment? It's the ultimate fear tactic.

In reality, Heaven and Hell as we know them are distractions. They are tools, narratives created to mask the true nature of what happens to us after we die. The afterlife isn't a place of moral judgment. It's a system, a machine, a vast and complex market where souls are the currency.

But who's running this market? Who's pulling the strings?

The Entities Behind the Curtain

To understand the afterlife market, you have to understand the entities that control it. These aren't the angels and demons you've read about in religious texts. These are far more ancient, far more powerful, and far more indifferent to human suffering. Some people call them archons, others call them interdimensional beings, but their names don't really matter. What matters is what they *do*.

These entities have existed since the beginning of time, long before humanity ever came into existence. They thrive on energy—specifically, the energy of souls. To them, souls are a resource, a form of currency that they use to sustain themselves and their reality. They're not gods. They're not demons, angels, or any kind of being that would care about your concept of morality. They don't give a fuck if you're good or bad, righteous or wicked. They're not interested in your prayers, your rituals, or your beliefs. They care about one thing: your soul and the energy it provides.

These entities operate like cosmic merchants, manipulating souls for their own purposes. Some trade souls like commodities, amassing vast collections of spiritual energy to increase their own power. Others harvest souls as fuel to maintain their own existence, feeding on the life force of the deceased to sustain their dimension. And still others bargain with souls, trading them for favors, power, or influence in this world and the next.

The Soul Harvesting Process

Let's talk about what happens when you die. I know it's a heavy subject, but it's one you've been lied to about for too long. Forget the tunnel of light. Forget the peaceful ascension. When you die, your soul—the very essence of who you are—immediately becomes part of the afterlife market.

The process begins with *soul harvesters*. These are beings tasked with collecting souls as they depart from the body. Sometimes, they appear as angels, guides, or comforting figures to trick the dying into willingly giving up their energy. Other times, they appear as dark shadows, dragging terrified souls away into the ether. Either way, their job is the same: to collect souls and deliver them to the market.

Once your soul is harvested, it doesn't just float off to some eternal rest. No, it's taken to a kind of *spiritual auction house*, where it's evaluated for its worth. Some souls are more valuable than others, depending on how much energy they carry. A soul that's lived a life of intense emotional experience—whether that's through love, trauma, or spiritual awakening—contains more energy, and therefore, is worth more in the afterlife market. A soul that's lived a dull, unremarkable existence might not fetch as high a price, but it's still a commodity.

Your soul is then put up for trade. The entities who control this market—those archon-like beings we talked about—begin the bidding process. They barter with each other for your soul, using it as leverage in their cosmic games. You might think your soul is your own, but once you're dead, it's just another piece in the vast machinery of the afterlife economy.

Soul Trafficking: The Darker Side of the Market

Not all souls are used for benevolent purposes—or even neutral ones. There's a dark underbelly to the afterlife market, a world of soul trafficking that is far more sinister than anything you could imagine. This is where the truly disturbing part comes in.

Certain entities specialize in what can only be described as *soul slavery.* These beings collect souls not to trade or consume them for energy, but to imprison and use them for their own twisted purposes. They bind souls, forcing them into endless cycles of servitude. Some souls are used as spiritual batteries, their energy slowly siphoned off over centuries or even millennia to power entire dimensions. Others are trapped in false realities—illusory paradises or hells—where they live out their existence in a manufactured dream state, unaware that they are being used as pawns in a much larger game.

These souls never get the release or peace they were promised. Instead, they become part of a never-ending cycle of exploitation, their energy harvested over and over again. And the worst part? Most souls never even realize what's happening to them.

Reincarnation as a Trap

This brings us to reincarnation—a concept that's been romanticized and twisted by spiritual teachings for centuries. You've heard the stories: you die, and if you haven't reached enlightenment, you get sent back to Earth to try again. Sounds reasonable, right? A second chance to get it right.

But here's the truth: reincarnation is just another tool of the afterlife market, a way to keep souls cycling through the system, producing energy indefinitely. When a soul has been sufficiently drained or used up, it's often sent back into the physical world for *renewal.* The soul re-enters a body, lives another life, collects more emotional and spiritual energy, and when it dies again, it's harvested all over again. Rinse and repeat.

This cycle can go on for eternity. You're not being given a second chance to ascend to a higher spiritual plane—you're being recycled, repurposed, and used as fuel for an interdimensional system that you never even knew existed. Reincarnation is not a gift; it's a trap. A way to keep the energy flowing and the afterlife market well-stocked with fresh souls.

The Soul Contracts: Did You Sign Up for This?

Here's another bombshell for you: many souls are bound to the afterlife market through *contracts*—spiritual agreements that you may not even remember making. These contracts can be formed in this life or in previous ones, through rituals, spiritual initiations, or even unknowingly through religious practices. In some cases, entities trick souls into agreeing to these contracts, binding them to the afterlife system in perpetuity.

Ever wonder why some people seem to suffer endlessly, no matter what they do? Why certain families seem cursed, generation after generation? It's possible they're caught in a web of soul contracts, bound to the market through agreements made long ago. These contracts can be incredibly difficult to break, and many souls end up trapped in the cycle of reincarnation or soul slavery because of them.

Can You Escape the Market?

Now, you're probably wondering, *Is there any way to escape this nightmare?* Is it possible to break free of the afterlife market and reclaim your soul?

The short answer is yes, but it's not easy.

Breaking free from the afterlife market requires an intense level of spiritual awareness and personal power. You have to become conscious of the forces that are trying to control your soul and learn how to protect yourself—both in life and in death. This means going beyond the teachings of mainstream religion and spiritual traditions, many of which are complicit in keeping you trapped in the cycle. You have to learn how to navigate the astral planes, how to shield your energy, and most importantly, how to break the contracts that bind you to the market.

There are ways to sever these contracts, to escape the clutches of the soul harvesters and the reincarnation trap. But it takes work. You have to unlearn everything you've been taught about the afterlife and start seeing it for what it really is: a system of control designed to keep you from realizing your true power as a spiritual being.

The Truth About Death

Death is not the end. It's not even the beginning. It's just another phase in a long, complicated system that you never signed up for. The afterlife is not a paradise waiting for you with open arms. It's a marketplace—a brutal, cutthroat economy where souls are traded, harvested, and used as currency in a cosmic game that most of us will never fully understand.

But here's the thing: now you *do* understand. Now you know what's really happening, and that knowledge is the first step toward freeing yourself. It's time to wake up. Time to reclaim your soul and break free from the system that's been exploiting you for lifetimes.

The afterlife market is real, and it's coming for you whether you believe in it or not.

The question is, what are you going to do about it?

| 5 |

Chapter Five: Opening the Doorways

So, now you know that the afterlife is nothing like you've been told, that shadow beings and astral parasites feed on your energy, and that your soul could be trapped in an endless cycle of exploitation. But what if I told you that all of this—the shadow figures, the soul harvesters, the interdimensional predators—can be summoned? That you could tear a hole in the veil between our reality and theirs, and they would come flooding through?

This is where things get dangerous. We're diving into the darkest, most forbidden knowledge that's been hidden from humanity for centuries: the ancient rituals that open doorways between dimensions, allowing beings from beyond to slip through. These rituals have been passed down through secret societies, occult orders, and rogue mystics who learned long ago that the veil between worlds is not as impenetrable as we'd like to think.

This isn't the kind of shit you play around with, though. We're talking about rituals that were deliberately buried because they *work*. The kind that, once set into motion, can't be undone. What steps across the threshold can't always be sent back. This is the path that takes you to the edge of madness, where the very fabric of reality tears apart and you're left staring into the abyss.

Are you ready for this?

The Thinness of the Veil

Before we get into the actual rituals, let's talk about the veil itself. Most people walk through life assuming the barrier between our world and others is unbreakable. That our reality is solid, impenetrable. But in truth, the veil between dimensions is fragile. It's thin, and there are places, people, and times when that veil becomes even thinner—when it's easier for things from the other side to come through.

Some cultures call these thin places "liminal spaces." They are crossroads, thresholds, or transitions—places where the physical and the metaphysical overlap. Graveyards, abandoned buildings, deep forests, even certain times of night, like the witching hour, when the veil is at its weakest. Ever felt a chill pass through you when you were standing somewhere alone at night? Ever sense something was just *off* in certain places? That's not your imagination. That's the veil thinning.

Now, some people don't have to wait for the veil to thin naturally. They've figured out how to *tear it open.*

Ancient Rituals: A Dangerous History

Rituals to summon beings from other dimensions have existed as long as humanity itself. From ancient Egypt to medieval Europe, people have tried—and sometimes succeeded—in opening doorways to the other side. The reasons varied: power, knowledge, revenge, or just pure curiosity. But regardless of intent, the outcome was often the same—chaos, madness, and death.

The Egyptians believed that certain rites could summon the gods, or more specifically, *the spirits of the dead*, to serve the living. Their rituals involved offerings, incantations, and blood sacrifices. But what most people don't know is that these rituals weren't just summoning the spirits of their ancestors. They were reaching into other dimensions, calling forth beings far older and more dangerous than they realized.

In medieval Europe, occult practitioners—some of whom later became known as witches or warlocks—developed rituals that blended Christian and pagan beliefs, creating powerful rites to summon angels and demons. These rituals were often written down in grimoires, books that were kept secret, hidden from the public because of their dangerous power. One such book, *The Lesser Key of Solomon*, outlines rituals to summon beings from beyond, beings that would grant the practitioner power, wealth, or knowledge—but always at a price. These weren't just demons in the religious sense. These were interdimensional entities, waiting on the other side for someone foolish enough to call them forth.

And the Sumerians, one of the oldest known civilizations, had rituals so dark that even mentioning them was believed to invite catastrophe. Their rites involved intricate symbols, sacrifices, and invocations to deities that were thought to exist beyond time and space. But these "deities" were more than just gods—they were ancient interdimensional forces that could manipulate reality itself.

Throughout history, the knowledge of these rituals has been passed down through secret societies—groups like the Freemasons, the Rosicrucians, and certain branches of the occult. These groups have kept these rites hidden, not out of a sense of morality, but out of self-preservation. They know what these rituals can do, and they know what happens when things go wrong.

Ritual One: The Blood Moon Gateway

One of the most dangerous and effective rituals to open a doorway between dimensions is known as the *Blood Moon Gateway*. This ritual has been passed down in whispered traditions, practiced by only the most daring—and desperate—of occultists. It requires precision, courage, and an absolute understanding that once the gateway is open, you have no control over what comes through.

Here's how it works:

What You'll Need:

- A mirror (this is your doorway)
- Blood (your own or an animal's—though using your own blood binds the ritual to you, making it far riskier)
- A candle made from human fat (this is an ingredient you'll need to procure through dark means)
- A black stone, preferably obsidian or onyx
- The exact time of a lunar eclipse (this is when the veil is thinnest)
- Incantations written in ancient Sumerian or Latin (depending on which version of the ritual you follow)

The Process:

1. **Prepare the Space:** Find a place where you won't be disturbed, preferably in an isolated area where the energy is already heavy—like a graveyard or an abandoned house. Set the mirror in the center of the space, facing east.
2. **Mark the Mirror:** Using your blood, draw the symbol of the key—a simple cross with a circle around it—on the surface of the mirror. This symbol has been used for centuries in rituals

meant to open doorways. It signifies the opening of the barrier between worlds.

3. **Light the Candle:** The candle made from human fat is a crucial part of the ritual. This isn't some witchy bullshit; the human fat is believed to resonate at a frequency that draws entities from other dimensions. Light the candle and place it in front of the mirror.

4. **The Black Stone:** Place the black stone at the base of the mirror. This acts as an anchor, keeping the doorway tied to this dimension. Without it, the portal could become unstable, and there's a chance that whatever comes through won't be bound to this plane.

5. **Recite the Incantation:** As the lunar eclipse reaches its peak, begin reciting the incantation. The words themselves aren't as important as the *intent* behind them. You are summoning something from the other side. You are inviting it in. The incantation is just the formal way of opening the door. What you're really doing is tearing a hole in the veil.

6. **Wait for the Sign:** Once the incantation is complete, the mirror will begin to change. Some people have reported seeing shadows moving within it. Others have seen faces, distorted and inhuman. The air will feel colder. Time may feel like it's slowing down. This is when the doorway is open.

What Comes Through: The Blood Moon Gateway doesn't just invite one specific entity. It opens a door to *whatever* is lurking on the other side. Some occultists have reported seeing shadow beings, others have encountered demonic figures, while some have felt the presence of something so powerful they couldn't describe it. The thing about opening doorways is that you have no control over what answers the call.

Once the doorway is open, it's nearly impossible to close. Some practitioners have reported hauntings that lasted for decades. Others lost their minds, claiming they could still feel the presence of the beings they summoned, even after they tried to close the portal. And some—well, they were never seen again.

Ritual Two: The Mirror of Abyssal Reflection

This next ritual is known as the *Mirror of Abyssal Reflection*, and it's even more dangerous because it doesn't just open a doorway—it allows whatever entity you summon to inhabit your reflection. That's right: your reflection becomes the entity's anchor to this world.

The ritual is rumored to have originated from an ancient Babylonian practice meant to communicate with gods and otherworldly forces. In modern times, it has been adapted by occult practitioners to contact and summon beings from alternate dimensions.

What You'll Need:

- A large black mirror (this must be perfectly polished, no flaws or cracks)
- Nightshade (a deadly plant with a long history in occult work)
- Three black candles
- A dagger with a silver blade
- A drop of your own blood
- A piece of obsidian or a black diamond (rare, but essential)

The Process:

1. **Set the Scene:** You must perform this ritual at midnight, the hour when the barrier between worlds is weakest. Place the black mirror in a completely dark room. Light the three black candles and arrange them in a triangle around the mirror.
2. **Nightshade and Blood:** Crush the nightshade into a fine powder and smear it across the surface of the mirror. Then, us-

ing the dagger, prick your finger and let a drop of blood fall onto the nightshade-covered mirror. This binds the mirror to your life force.

3. **The Obsidian Anchor:** Place the piece of obsidian or black diamond at the base of the mirror. This acts as a tether, ensuring the entity remains bound to the reflection and cannot step into your physical world. It's a precaution, but in many cases, it's been said to fail.

4. **Recite the Invocation:** There is no specific incantation for this ritual; instead, you must speak from your soul. The invocation is personal, designed to call forth the entity you seek. Be warned, though—this is a dangerous moment. The entity you call may not be the one that answers.

5. **Look Into the Mirror:** Once the invocation is complete, stare directly into the mirror. You will begin to see changes in your reflection—distortions, movements that don't match your own. This is the entity arriving. Once it has fully manifested, it will live within your reflection, bound to you.

What Happens Next: The danger of this ritual lies in the fact that you can never escape the entity once it's summoned. Every time you look into a reflective surface—whether it's a mirror, a window, or even water—you'll see it. It will be there, watching you, mimicking your movements, waiting for an opportunity to slip through. Over time, it will grow stronger, and eventually, it may take over entirely.

Some occultists who have performed this ritual have reported being possessed by the entities they summoned. Others claimed that they could feel the presence of the entity constantly, even when they weren't looking in the mirror. And some—well, their reflections were found shattered, as though something had broken through.

The Consequences of Tearing the Veil

Opening doorways between dimensions is no game. These ancient rituals are not for the curious or the faint of heart. The beings that answer your call do not come with good intentions. They are predators, interdimensional forces that see humanity as little more than playthings or food. Once you open the door, it can never fully be closed again.

You might think you're calling for power, for knowledge, or for revenge. But what comes through that doorway is beyond your control. Once you've invited them in, they stay—feeding on your fear, manipulating your thoughts, and slowly, steadily, pulling you further into their reality.

The veil between worlds is fragile. You can tear it open if you know how. But remember this: once you open that door, you can never be sure what will come through.

And whatever does—whether it's a shadow being, an ancient demon, or something far worse—will never leave you alone.

CONCLUSION: LIVING WITH THE SHADOWS

By now, you've seen beyond the comforting lies we've all been fed about reality. We've ripped apart the stories of Heaven and Hell, cracked open the myths of a peaceful afterlife, and exposed the horrifying truth: that everything we thought we knew about the spiritual world is nothing but a well-crafted illusion. The truth is darker, more complex, and far more terrifying than most people can handle.

The spirits, entities, and dimensions we've explored aren't fairy tales—they're real. And they're closer than you think.

You've learned that the shadow people lurking just outside your vision aren't figments of your imagination. They are interdimensional predators, watching, waiting, feeding on your fear. You've come to understand that astral parasites can latch onto your energy, slowly draining you of life until you're a hollow version of yourself. You've discovered that the afterlife is not a place of eternal rest or torment but a market where souls are traded, harvested, and consumed by ancient forces you never knew existed. And if you dare to dig deeper, you've been shown how ancient rituals can tear open the veil between dimensions, inviting unspeakable entities into your life—entities that may never leave.

If you're still reading, you're one of the few who can handle the truth. But knowing the truth is only the beginning. The real challenge is living with it.

The Unseen War

What you have to understand now is that the world you live in isn't the safe, predictable place it seems to be. There is an unseen war raging all around you—a battle between light and dark, between dimensional forces vying for control, and you're caught in the middle. Every time you feel that chill up your spine, every time you sense something watching you in the dark, that's the battlefield brushing up against your reality.

You're not just a passive observer in this war, though. Whether you like it or not, you're a participant. Your energy, your soul, your fear—these are the resources these entities fight over. And now that you've peeled back the layers and seen the truth, you have a choice to make. You can either close this book, walk away, and pretend that none of this exists. You can go back to the comfortable lies, telling yourself that ghosts aren't real, that spirits are harmless, that the afterlife is a peaceful paradise.

Or, you can face the truth head-on and arm yourself for what comes next.

Reclaiming Your Power

You've learned that knowledge is the key to reclaiming your power. These entities, these forces from other dimensions, thrive on ignorance. They manipulate you through your fear, your lack of awareness, and your willingness to believe in the comforting stories you've been told. But once you see through the lies, they lose some of their power over you.

The first step in reclaiming your power is acknowledging that these entities exist, that they are real, and that they are here. The second step is learning how to protect yourself. We've touched on some of the ways you can do this—strengthening your aura, performing cleansing rituals, severing contracts that bind you to the afterlife market—but the most important thing you can do is stay vigilant. The more aware you are, the harder it is for these entities to latch onto you.

Remember: fear is their food. The more you let it control you, the more power they have over you. So don't give them that power. When you feel them watching, when you sense them lurking, recognize it for what it is—an attempt to feed. Refuse to give in. Stand firm. Protect your energy, your mind, and your soul.

Walking the Edge

Living with this knowledge means walking a fine line. You'll start to notice things that other people don't—the shadow at the edge of your vision, the energy drain after a long day, the unsettling presence in your home. You'll feel the thinness of the veil, understand the way certain places make your skin crawl, and be aware of the subtle ways these forces try to influence your life. You'll see the world for what it really is—a web of interdimensional connections, with your energy at the center of it all.

But there's a danger in walking this path. Once you see the truth, there's no going back. You can't unsee the shadow beings, the parasites, the soul harvesters. They'll always be there, lurking just beyond the edges of your perception, waiting for a moment of weakness. You'll have to stay vigilant, constantly protecting yourself from the entities that want to consume your energy and drag you into their world.

Survival in the New Reality

So how do you survive in this new reality? It's simple, but not easy.

1. **Strengthen Your Spirit:** Your energy is your most valuable asset. Strengthen it through meditation, spiritual practices, or energy work. Keep your aura strong, and don't let these entities find any cracks to exploit.

2. **Stay Grounded:** One of the best defenses against these interdimensional forces is staying grounded in your physical reality. Don't let yourself be pulled too deeply into the metaphysical without anchoring yourself in the here and now. These entities thrive on pulling you away from your physical body and trapping you in the astral realm.

3. **Set Boundaries:** Just because these entities exist doesn't mean they have to have access to you. Set strong spiritual boundaries. Use protection spells, cleansing rituals, and crystals if that's your thing. But most importantly, use your mind. Mental strength is your greatest weapon.

4. **Educate Yourself:** The more you know about these forces, the better equipped you'll be to deal with them. Read, study, learn from those who have walked this path before you. But be cautious—knowledge comes with responsibility. The more you learn, the more these entities will notice you.

5. **Live Fearlessly:** Fear is their greatest weapon. It's what gives them power. If you can live fearlessly, if you can face these forces head-on without letting terror control you, you've already won half the battle.

The Final Truth

In the end, the final truth is this: reality is far stranger and more terrifying than we've been led to believe. The entities we've explored in this book—the shadow beings, the astral parasites, the interdimensional predators—they are all part of the hidden machinery of the universe, operating just outside the range of our perception. They are ancient, powerful, and hungry. But they are not invincible.

You have more power than you realize. Your soul, your energy, your very existence is valuable—not just to these entities, but to yourself. You have the ability to reclaim your power, to protect yourself, and to navigate this new, terrifying reality with strength and courage.

The shadows may always be there, but so will you.

The veil is thin, but you're not helpless. Now that you know the truth, it's up to you to decide what to do with it.

Welcome to the real world.

Demetri Welsh is an unapologetic force in the world of metaphysics, known for pushing boundaries and tearing apart the veil between the seen and the unseen. A renowned psychic reader, energy worker, and author, Demetri's work dives into the dark corners of existence—where science meets spirit, and reality crumbles into chaos. His books explore the hidden realms of the paranormal, the occult, and the forbidden knowledge that most are too afraid to confront. With a lifetime of personal experience in spiritual warfare, shadow work, and the metaphysical unknown, Demetri's work challenges conventional beliefs and ignites controversy with every page.

You can find his services and more of his uncensored musings exclusively on Fiverr at www.fiverr.com/rawveganpsychic.